W9-AOZ-713

ADMITTING MISTAKES

DATE DUE		
MAY 2 3 2005 SEP 0 3 2011		
JUN 3 0 2006		
JUL 1 7 2006		
AUG 1 2 2006		
AUG 1 6 2006		
JUL 2 2 2009		
JUL 2 9 2009		
JUN 3 0 2011		

A.R. 1.6

Courteous Kids

Admitting Mistakes

By Janine Amos   Illustrated by Annabel Spenceley
Consultant Rachael Underwood

Gareth Stevens Publishing
A WORLD ALMANAC EDUCATION GROUP COMPANY

Please visit our web site at: www.garethstevens.com
For a free color catalog describing Gareth Stevens Publishing's
list of high-quality books and multimedia programs,
call 1-800-542-2595 (USA) or 1-800-387-3178 (Canada).
Gareth Stevens Publishing's fax: (414) 332-3567.

Library of Congress Cataloging-in-Publication Data

Amos, Janine.
    Admitting mistakes / by Janine Amos; illustrated by Annabel Spenceley.
        p. cm. — (Courteous kids)
    Includes bibliographical references.
    Summary: Provides examples and tips for making things better when one
has made a mistake that upsets someone else.
    ISBN 0-8368-3168-3 (lib. bdg.)
    1. Truthfulness and falsehood—Juvenile literature. [1. Honesty.
2. Conduct of life.] I. Spenceley, Annabel, ill. II. Title.
BJ1421.A35   2002
177'.1—dc21   2002017714

This edition first published in 2002 by
Gareth Stevens Publishing
A World Almanac Education Group Company
330 West Olive Street, Suite 100
Milwaukee, Wisconsin 53212 USA

Gareth Stevens editor: JoAnn Early Macken
Cover Design: Katherine A. Goedheer

This edition © 2002 by Gareth Stevens, Inc. First published by Cherrytree Press,
a subsidiary of Evans Brothers Limited. © 1997 by Cherrytree (a member of the
Evans Group of Publishers), 2A Portman Mansions, Chiltern Street, London
W1M 1LE, United Kingdom. This U.S. edition published under license from
Evans Brothers Limited. Additional end matter © 2002 by Gareth Stevens, Inc.

Printed in the United States of America

1 2 3 4 5 6 7 8 9 06 05 04 03 02

Note to Parents and Teachers

The questions that appear in **boldface** type can be used to initiate
discussion with your children or class. Encourage them to think of
possible answers before continuing with the story.

Emma and Dad

The kitchen is a mess.

Dad is going to clean it up.

He washes the dishes.
He sweeps the floor.

He clears off the table.
He throws away all the trash.

When the cleaning is done, Emma comes in.
"Where's my project?" she asks.
"It was on the table."

Dad looks at Emma.
Then he looks at the trash can.

"I made a mistake, Emma," Dad says.
"I put your project in the trash can."

Emma is upset, so Dad gives her a hug.
How does Dad feel?

"I'm sorry," says Dad. "That project was important to you, wasn't it?"

Emma nods her head.
How does she feel?

"Why don't we find somewhere safe
to keep your projects?" says Dad.
"How about in that drawer?"

"Yes!" Emma agrees.
"We'll need to empty it first," Dad tells her.

15

"Let's do it now!" says Emma.
"Okay," says Dad.

Emma makes another project.

Dad cleans up the kitchen again.

Ann and Kadeem

"Chug! Chug! I'm building
a tractor," says Ann.

Ann works hard until the tractor is finished.
Then she looks in the toy box for a driver.

Kadeem comes to build a train.

He picks up Ann's tractor and pulls it apart
so he can use pieces of it for his train.

"Hey! Where's my tractor?" Ann asks.
"I used it to make my train," Kadeem answers.
"I didn't know you still wanted it."

24

How do you think Ann feels?
How does Kadeem feel?
What could they do?

"You can play with my train," Kadeem says.

"But I want a tractor," Ann tells him.

Kadeem thinks hard.

"We could make a new tractor," he says.

"Yes," Ann agrees, "with red wheels!"

Together, Ann and Kadeem build a new tractor.

Sometimes, people make mistakes. Some mistakes upset other people. If you make this kind of mistake, admit it. Tell the other person what you did. Explain what happened. It might help the person understand. Try to think of a way to make things better.

More Books to Read

The Culprit Was a Fly. Lisa Funari-Willever (Angel Publications)

Foggy Plays Soccer. Jonathan London (Viking)

Oops! I Made a Mistake. Susan Hood (Econo-Clad Books)